Antigua Black

Gregson Davis was born in Antigua, the third child of a family of seven children. Both his parents were teachers, and he attended his aunt's elementary school in his own backyard. At age 15 Gregson was awarded a scholarship from Harvard University, which was then supplemented by a Mill Reef Club scholarship, enabling him to enroll at Harvard in 1956 toward the A.B. in Classics. He took a Ph.D. in Comparative Literature at University of California, Berkeley, and is currently Assistant Professor of Classics and Comparative Literature at Stanford, with a special interest in Caribbean literature, culture, and history. In progress is a translation of the work of Aimé Césaire, the famous Martiniquan poet.

DAVIS, Gregson. Antigua black; portrait of an island people. Photos by Margo Davis. Scrimshaw, 1973. 141p plates il map 73-78447. 27.50. ISBN 0-912020-30-X

CHOICE   JAN/74
History, Geography & Travel

Latin America

This stunningly beautiful book is a sensitive, compassionate portrait of the rural Antiguan people, caught in transition from a sugar-plantation society to an equally repressive one based on tourism. Directly perceived photographs by Margo Davis are complemented by her husband Gregson's text. He makes liberal use of contemporary sources to explain the background of slavery on which the Antiguan plantation system is based and shows how internal dissensions such as the conspiracy of 1735 shaped both the island's economy and its captives. Old color prints, beautifully reproduced, provide a visual account fully as informative and impressive as the photographs. Nonetheless, the text is so beautifully written that it must be given equal billing with all the pictures. *Antigua black* is an exemplary job of book production, recommended for both its subject matter and the authors' approach to that material. Suitable for both graduate and undergraduate libraries.

A pineapple; in Goncalo de Oviedo, *La hystoria general de las Indias*, Salamanca, 1547

ANTIGUA BLACK

Portrait of an Island People

Photographs by Margo Davis

Text by Gregson Davis

SCRIMSHAW PRESS   SAN FRANCISCO

1973

Engraving Credits:

p. 49: *English Harbour, Antigua. From
Great George Fort, Monk's Hill.* Drawn by
J. Johnson. Engraved by T. Fielding. London,
Published 1 May 1827, by T. & G. Underwood,
Fleet Street.

p. 60: *View near St. John's Antigua. From
Gamble's.* Drawn by J. Johnson. Engraved by
G. Reeve. London, Published July 1st 1829,
by Smith, Elder & Co. Cornhill.

The engravings on pp. 51-59 are from William
Clark's *Ten Views in the Island of Antigua.*
Published by Thomas Clay, Ludgate Hill,
London 1823.

*All engravings are from the Collection of
Mr. and Mrs. Paul Mellon.*

————•·•————

Poetry on pp. 48 and 106 from *Islands,* by
Edward Brathwaite, © Oxford University Press,
1969. Reprinted by permission of the publisher.

for the people of Antigua

Old Copper

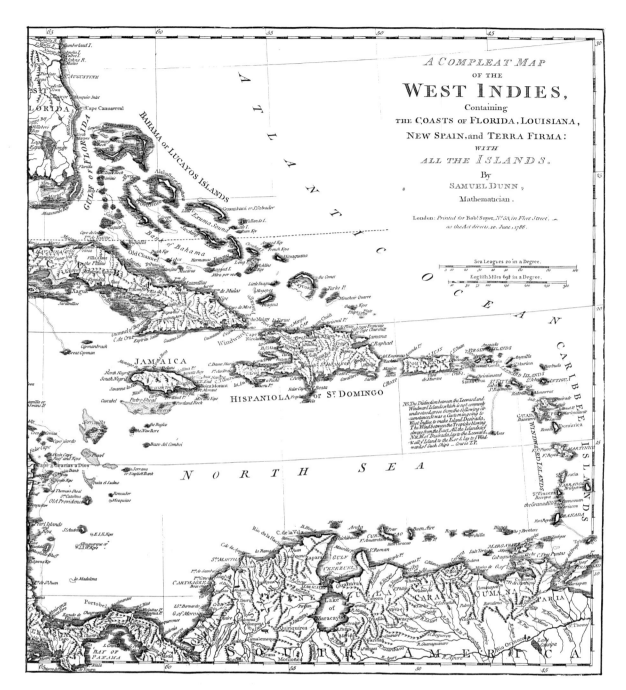

A complete map of the West Indies containing the Coasts of Florida, Louisiana, New Spain and Terra Firma with all the Islands by Samuel Dunn, Mathematician, London, printed for Robert Sayer, No. 53 in Fleet Street, 10 June 1786. (Stanford University Central Map Collection)

A new and accurate map of the Island of Antigua or Antego, taken from Surveys and adjusted by Astron'l. Observations; containing all the Towns, Parish Churches, Forts, Castles, Windmills, Roads, etc. by Eman. Bowen. (1750?)

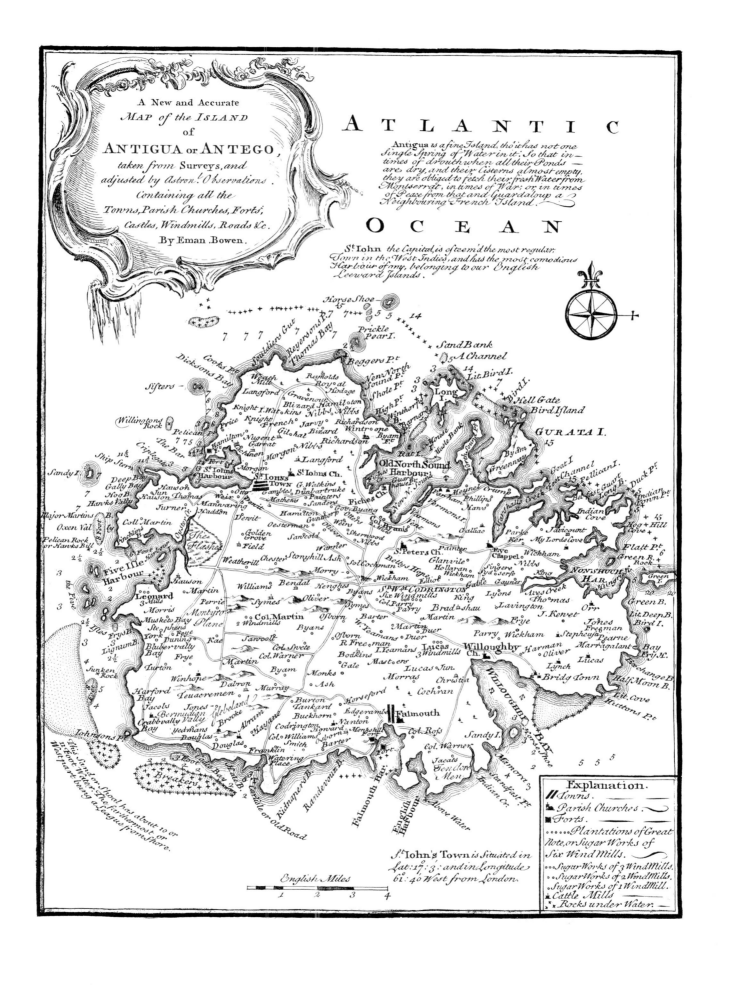

A New and Accurate
MAP of the ISLAND
of
ANTIGUA or ANTEGO,
taken from Surveys, and
adjusted by Astron.l Observations.
Containing all the
Towns, Parish Churches, Forts,
Castles, Windmills, Roads &c.
By Eman. Bowen.

A T L A N T I C

Antigua is a fine Island, tho' it has not one
single Spring of Water in it: So that in —
times of drouth when all their Ponds —
are dry, and their Cisterns almost empty,
they are obliged to fetch their fresh Water from
Montserrat, in times of War: or in times
of Peace from that and Guardaloup a
Neighbouring French Island.

O C E A N

St. Iohn the Capital, is esteem'd the most regular
Town in the West Indies, and has the most comodious
Harbour of any, belonging to our English
Leeward Islands.

St. Iohn's Town is situated in
Lat: 17°: 3: and in Longitude
61: 40 West from London.

English Miles

1   2   3   4

Explanation.
Towns.
Parish Churches.
Forts.
Plantations of Great
Note, or Sugar Works of
Six Wind Mills.
Sugar Works of 3 Wind Mills.
Sugar Works of 2 Wind Mills.
Sugar Works of 1 Wind Mill.
Cattle Mills
Rocks under Water.

Foreword

We offer on the pages of this book a straightforward view of rural Antigua. It is
not the Antigua of congested city streets, hectic supermarkets, busy bureaucrats and oil
refineries, nor the sentimentalized Antigua of the folklorists, nor yet the paradisiacal
Antigua of the tourist brochures. It is the Antigua that we all take for granted but
seldom observe closely with tenderness and admiration: the Antigua of village yards
and tilled plots, where the descendants of slaves—Antigua blacks—labor with strength
and ingenuity to extract a life of dignity and meaning from an eroded landscape of
unfulfilled promises and fragmented hopes. Our view is, we hope, steady and
compassionate.

Antigua Black is essentially a book of photographs. What take precedence in our
view are the visual elements—black and white photographs and color engravings. The
images came first and generated the concept of the book; the words came after and are
meant to complement the images, to provide background information in an unobtrusive
way. Aesthetic delight is enhanced by an awareness of the cultural roots of the
transplanted people who appear in the prints. For our viewers we offer an
impressionistic text which seeks to fix, without polemic, certain decisive moments
in Antiguan history—those moments that we see as crucial to any deeper understanding
of the black experience in the New World. The text also incorporates several excerpts
from rare books and ancient documents which shed light on obscure facets of
Antiguan history, such as the events of the Antigua Conspiracy of 1735.

Antigua is a microcosm of that awesome experience. But even a tiny cosmos of 108
square miles has its hidden valleys, unfamiliar faces, forgotten backyards,
surprising dimensions. We hope that *Antigua Black* will reveal some neglected aspects
of our island's present and past both to ourselves and to others—those who know
us in part already and those who will come to know us more profoundly in the future.

Gregson and Margo Davis

ABORIGINAL
ANTIGUA

The dusty road to Shirley Heights, a promontory in southern Antigua, struggles upward through stubborn thickets of thorn and cactus. On either side, patches of red soil peer, like bloodshot eyes, through lattice screens of acacia with their tough, gnarled twigs and yellow blossoms. Toward the summit, tall Antigua Pride and wild cherries jostle with the acacia bushes for survival among the outcrops of rock and the eroded slopes. Once on the windy summit, the sun-pummelled climber can pick out tiny, motley spots far below that meander slowly between dagger plants and prickly pear clumps—these turn out to be goats browsing on the steep, desiccated cliffs.

To westward, amidst the dryness and the desolation, ruins of old stone fortresses stand in the foreground as eerie witnesses to former British imperial might, along with rusting black cannon, empty magazines, and tombstone monuments to soldiers who perished in yellow fever epidemics. In the background the reconstructed barracks of Nelson's Dockyard lie in grey quiescence, protected by a land-locked harbor. To eastward, and also in the background, the deeply indented shimmering cove of "Indian Creek" conjures up the phantoms of Carib and Arawak canoes. Besides the steady drone of the wind and the distant plashing of a wave, the only sounds to reach the ear are the scuttle of a ground lizard or mongoose through the underbrush and the busy whirr of an occasional hummingbird.

On these desiccated heights one can readily reconstruct the uneven triangle formed by the Indians who once fished the bays below, the European colonizers who planted their impregnable defences on superior ground, and the African slaves who transported the stone and hauled the cannon. The story of the human intersection is unintelligible without the older story of the land and sea that surrounds it. So it is with the land and sea that we shall begin.

The calm waters of the Caribbean Sea are bounded on the south and west by the two Americas, on the north and east by an archipelago of islands that stretches from the Florida peninsula to the mouth of the Orinoco River in Venezuela. Roughly one-half of the stretch comprises the Greater Antilles: Cuba, Jamaica, Haiti, Santo Domingo, and Puerto Rico; the remainder constitutes the sinuous curve of the Lesser Antilles with its "leeward" and "windward" folds.

"Leeward" and "windward," like so many other place-names in the "West Indies," are part of our legacy of confused nomenclature. The terms have been used to refer to different island groupings at different periods in history, and the present denotation was not firmly established until the nineteenth century. Firmly ignoring these artificial categories, the topography of the Lesser Antilles shows a clear contrast between an inner and an outer arc of islands. The inner arc with its typical volcanic cones and lush vegetation is by far the larger, including among others within its sweep, the "leeward" islands of St. Kitts, Nevis and Montserrat, and the "windward" islands of Dominica, Martinique, St. Lucia, St. Vincent, and Grenada. By contrast, the smaller outer arc of Antigua, Barbuda, Anguilla and Anegada (all "leeward" islands) is mainly of limestone formation and is typically low-lying and less thickly wooded. By its pivotal position, the outer arc of "Limestone Caribbees" represents a kind of shield to the buffets of the Atlantic Ocean.

The contrasting features of the two arcs are juxtaposed in the French island of Guadeloupe, whose western half, being rugged and mountainous, belongs to the volcanic arc, while its eastern half, separated by a narrow isthmus, displays the overall flatness characteristic of the "Limestone Caribbees." On a far less dramatic scale, the neighboring island of Antigua also reflects these same contrasts. To the eye of the mariner approaching the island, the relative flatness of Antigua's northeastern (limestone) shores is counterbalanced by the bulge of hills on its southwestern (volcanic) coast.

Antigua means "old, ancient." Christopher Columbus, when he chose the name, was paying tribute to a church in Seville which bore a medieval fresco of the Madonna—Santa Maria la Antigua. "Antigua," formerly an epithet, has long since drifted from its syntactic moorings and now evokes images of distant antiquity. Yet, measured by the yardstick of geological time, "Antigua" is another of those ironic misnomers with which our history is replete. The geological record indicates that the island is probably no older than the Upper Oligocene period—relatively recent by comparison with the rest of the archipelago. By the time of Antigua's appearance roughly 40 million years ago, the main cordillera (or mountain chain) of the Greater, and part of the Lesser, Antilles had already been formed, albeit by dint of prolonged, intermittent building activity that had commenced much earlier.

Antigua's present demeanor of calmness, like that of the Caribbean Sea itself, is deceptive. In the dim reaches of the Upper Oligocene the island, or what is now the hilly southwestern end of it, was formed in a series of violent volcanic eruptions. Depositions attendant upon this activity created the major portions of the "Barbuda Bank," a submarine platform on which the islands of Antigua and Barbuda both sit.

Consensus of expert opinion holds that the land and the sea levels of Antigua have fluctuated continually since the island's fiery birth. Volcanism declined, but sporadic outbursts occurred frequently enough to produce the layered tuffs of the central plain. In subsequent millennia large portions of the island slowly submerged, while by a contrary process the limestone areas of the so-called "Antigua formation" surfaced. The geological events of the Miocene and more recent times are subjects of controversy, but it appears that, along with considerable erosion and planing-down of the land surface, tilting and faulting in the southwestern mountains created the effects visible today. The sharply defined topography which we see now is only the most recent configuration of a land surface which has shifted many times in the geological past. (Martin-Kaye, 1959, p. 25)

Today's Antigua displays a highly indented perimeter with myriad bays and coves, of which those on the leeward (or Caribbean) side are calm enclaves of white sand, while those on the windward (or Atlantic) side are choppy and wind-battered. Within the perimeter the limestone escarpment of the northeast is divorced from the volcanic bulge of the southwest by an intervening central plain, so that the island's topography falls into three clear segments.

Pre-Columbian Antigua was, of course, strikingly different in its flora and fauna from the island today. Before the massive destruction of the rain forests by Europeans, the island was much more lush and thickly wooded. Evergreen forests of red and white cedar—now confined to straggling bands in the southwest—once covered much of the low-lying plains and supported several species of large agouti-like rodents which are long extinct. Along the few creeks grew noble stands of whitewood. On the shores and offshore islands, iguanas roamed in plenty. But above all, the island was full of colorful birds. The more spectacular of these, such as the parrot, have long since vanished. Especially impressive to the eye must have been the prehistoric fauna of the marshlands along the leeward coasts. These marshes were graced by the presence of roseate flamingos *(Phoenicopterus ruber)* and the nearby beaches and offshore islands sported colonies of Audubon's Shearwater. All defunct.

Who were the original "natives" of the Caribbean archipelago before the encroachment of the Europeans and the transplantation of the blacks? Meager vestiges of the aboriginal Amerindian peoples survived the genocidal practices of the invaders—a few hundred in the windward islands of Dominica, St. Lucia and St. Vincent. Caribbean archaeologists now disagree about earlier "Paleo-Indians," "Meso-Indians," and "Neo-Indians" and their respective dates of occupation of the archipelago. As our knowledge increases, the earlier accepted date for the arrival of man from South America—the first century A.D.—has been abandoned, and scholars are now saying that Paleo-Indians had already reached the Antilles by the fifth millennium B.C. (Cruxent and Rouse, 1969). However shadowy and fragmentary may be our present picture of early man in the Caribbean, we do know quite a bit about the later "Indians" whom Columbus and his men encountered. They belonged to two main groups, the Arawaks and the Caribs, both of which migrated to the islands from the South American mainland. The ethnohistory of the Lesser Antilles in aboriginal times is well summarized by the geographer, David R. Harris:

An Indian Habitation; in Gonçalo de Oviedo,
La hystoria general de las Indias, Salamanca,
1547

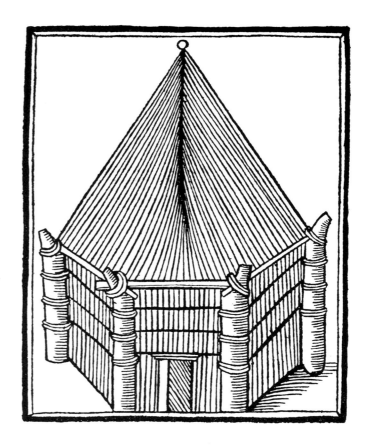

The Lesser Antilles appear to have been first settled by "Neo-Indians" from
South America who were probably ancestors of the Arawak-speaking peoples whom
Columbus encountered in the Greater Antilles. They migrated from the Vene-
zuelan mainland, by way of the Paria peninsula and Trinidad, and spread north
and west, through the small islands and out into the Greater Antilles. . . .

The Arawaks were agricultural folk who practiced shifting cultivation and
brought with them from the South American mainland a considerable range
of crop plants. They evidently occupied the Lesser Antilles for many generations
before their peaceful tenure of the islands was disrupted by the invasion of
Carib-speaking Indians. The Caribs were agriculturalists like their predecessors
and also migrated from South America. They probably occupied the southernmost
islands about 1000 A.D. and moved gradually north, supplanting the Arawaks
as they did so. By 1493 when Columbus, returning to his new-found "Indies," discovered and explored the islands that lie northwards from Dominica, the Caribs had
already expelled the Arawaks from the Leeward Islands and were raiding their
villages in eastern Puerto Rico. The successful expulsion of the Arawaks from
the Lesser Antilles was due to the Caribs' superior fighting prowess and their reputation for cannibalism, a combination that later discouraged the Spanish from
attempting permanent settlement of the islands. . . .

View of English Harbour from Shirley Heights

Despite the contrast between peaceful Arawak and warlike Carib that so impressed
Columbus and his successors in the West Indies there was little difference in the
economy of the two peoples. Both depended for their livelihood on a combination of shifting cultivation, hunting, and fishing. They raised essentially the
same complex of crops derived from the tropical American mainland; they employed
the same methods of fishing; and they hunted small game with the aid of dogs,
which were their only important domestic animal. Both were maritime
peoples making full and varied use of the warm seas that washed their island
shores, and the skill they displayed in and on the water, diving, swimming, and
navigating their large seagoing canoes, astonished the early Spanish explorers.

(Harris, 1965, pp. 71-73)

As far as Antigua is concerned, the truly indigenous people were the Arawaks.
These people were extremely skilled exploiters of the insular niche that they chose to
inhabit. They supplemented their fabulous diet of seafood, including delectable
sea-turtles, with cultivated crops like the sweet potato, cassava and maize. Living
in villages under the headship of *caciques* they practiced their arts of pottery and
weaving, both of which they had developed to a very high level.

Some idea of how the Arawaks appeared to the invading Europeans may be gained
from the following contemporary account taken from Christopher Columbus's
invaluable *Journal:*

And all those whom I did see were youths, so that I did not see one who was
over thirty years of age; they were very well built, with very handsome bodies and
very good faces. Their hair is coarse almost like the hairs of a horse's tail and
short; they wear their hair down over their eyebrows, except for a few strands
behind, which they wear long and never cut. Some of them are painted black, and

they are the colour of the people of the Canaries, neither black nor white, and some of them are painted white and some red and some in any colour that they find. Some of them paint their faces, some their whole bodies, some only the eyes, and some only the nose. They do not bear arms or know them, for I showed to them swords and they took them by the blade and cut themselves through ignorance. They have no iron. Their spears are certain reeds, without iron, and some of these have a fish tooth at the end, while others are pointed in various ways. They are all generally fairly tall, good looking and well proportioned. I saw some who bore marks of wounds on their bodies, and I made signs to them to ask how this came about, and they indicated to me that people came from other islands, which are near, and wished to capture them, and they defended themselves. And I believed and still believe that they come here from the mainland to take them for slaves. They should be good servants and of quick intelligence, since I see that they very soon say all that is said to them, and I believe that they would easily be made Christians, for it appeared to me that they had no creed.   (Jane, 1968, p. 74)

Ethnographically crude though this may be, we can already discern the lineaments of an ideology that lead to the abortive enslavement and eventual destruction of the Amerindians.

To what degree are the black Antiguans of today aware of the Amerindian past? Hardly at all. Visible reminders of the aborigines do exist in the form of rare genetic traits affecting hair, complexion, and phenotype; but these are tenuous and provoke little interest. The archaeologist's spade has so far unearthed some impressive artifacts (pottery, cassava griddles, etc.) but these are mainly in foreign museums and consequently inaccessible to the general Antiguan public. The major point of contact for us, as Antiguans, with the indigenous population has been the fantasy world of elementary schoolbooks—at least for those of us who recall the *Nelson's Readers* that selectively shaped our images of the past.

We are still occasionally haunted by the bold images from these books: on the one hand, the fat Arawak who is always horizontal, prostrate in a hammock (his own invention) and smoking tobacco (his own invention); on the other, the Carib, ever-vertical and alert, brandishing a spear from his canoe, ready to attack and then devour his decadent victim. In these stereotypes— so central to the simplistic universe of the colonial reading-book—awesome lessons were subliminally imprinted on our childish minds. Somehow the dispossession and extermination of the Amerindian disappeared behind the screen of tobacco smoke exhaled by the Arawak at his siesta and the pile of human bones left by his Carib rival.

In his second voyage to the Indies in 1493 Columbus re-entered the Caribbean on a Sunday near the towering island he called (appropriately enough) "Dominica" and, with the friendly support of the northeast tradewinds, proceeded to "discover" most of the Leeward Islands. From the extant diary of his physician, Dr. Chanca, we have a vivid account of the Spaniards' encounter with both Amerindian groups, and their wonder at the strange flora and fauna of the Antilles. Their unfortunate introduction to the manchineel—a seductive but toxic plant that covers much of the shoreline—is typical of their curiosity before the exotic:

On this island [Marie-Galante] the trees were amazingly dense, and were of a great variety of species known to none of us. Some were in fruit, some in flower, and all therefore were green. We found one tree, like a laurel but not so large, the leaves of which had the finest scent of clove that I have ever smelt. I think it must have been a species of laurel. There were wild fruit of different kinds, which some rashly tried. But no sooner did they taste them than their faces swelled, growing so inflamed and painful that they almost went out of their minds. They cured themselves with cold compresses. We found no people on this island, nor any sign of them, and believed it to be uninhabited. (Cohen, 1969, p. 132)

An Indian hammock; in Gonçalo de Oviedo, *La hystoria general de las Indias*, Salamanca, 1547.

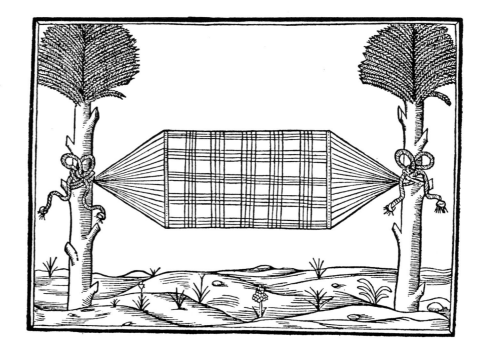

According to the historian, Samuel Eliot Morison, the Spanish flotilla sailed past the southern end of the island of Antigua, most probably in the vicinity of Shirley Heights (Morison and Obregon, 1964, p. 129). The Admiral did not stop, as we know from Dr. Chanca's tantalizing words:

> . . . in the evening we sighted another island [Santa Maria la Redonda] and at nightfall found some shoals close to it, for fear of which we dropped anchor, not daring to go further until daylight. Next morning another island [Santa Maria la Antigua] of considerable size appeared. We visited none of these, being anxious to relieve those who had been left on Hispaniola . . . (Cohen, 1969, pp. 137-138)

Columbus, suffering from insomnia and obsessed with a sense of his destined mission

Indians flee in fear of Columbus; in Giuliano Dati, *Isole Trovate Nuovamente Per El Re di Spagna*, Florence, 1495.

as "Christ-bearer," must have had haunting associations with the Virgin and Seville as the hills and deeply indented bays of southwestern Antigua rose into view on his right. He had already christened several islands en route after shrines of the Madonna in Spain, such as Santa Maria de Guadalupe and Santa Maria de Monserrat. He was thus following his own recent whimsy in calling the new island Santa Maria la Antigua "after a famous miracle-working Virgin in Seville Cathedral, before whom he is said to have prayed a few days before his voyage began." (Morison, 1942, p. 410) But if the Virgin of Seville accorded Christopher Columbus the miracle of a successful voyage to the New World, she apparently did not extend her favors to the Spaniards in the settlement of the island which is her namesake. Antigua has never been Spanish in anything but name, and the ruined forts which decorate Shirley Heights are monuments of British rather than Spanish colonial might.

Carib Indian Girl, Dominica

TRANSPLANTATION

The stern of a ship; detail of a woodcut in
Bernhard von Breydenbach, *Peregrinationes in
Terram Sanctam*, Mainz, 1486

The Spaniards, like the Caribs, never made Santa Maria la Antigua their home. The human vacuum created by the uprooting of the Arawaks by the Caribs was not filled until the English established a colony in 1632. By that time, the Arawak name for the island was already lost. Although the island, as far as we know, remained uninhabited by man for at least a century and a half, it was undergoing momentous ecological changes which had been set in motion first by the aborigines, then greatly accelerated by European freebooters, buccaneers and adventurers, who made sporadic visits to its wooded shore. (Harris, 1965, pp. 79-83)

The Arawaks had cleared some of the virgin rain forest by their practice of shifting cultivation, which involved the time-honored technique of burning a wooded plot before planting it in root crops, such as manioc, tania, and sweet potatoes. Presumably they denuded some portions of the windward peninsulas in this way, but the scope of their impact on the Antiguan vegetation was relatively restricted. Engaged primarily in hunting, fishing and gathering, they probably achieved an equilibrium in relation to their environmen, whereby they did not exhaust its resources.

During the interlude of calm which reigned in Antigua throughout the sixteenth century, the island's resources were intermittently tapped in similar ways by both Carib and European interlopers. Since the island has a plethora of bays and coves, both groups used it as a convenient haven and a source of victuals. The Caribs dropped in to persue wild game, such as agouti and iguana, and to fish the teeming reefs; the Europeans also came to hunt and garner medicinal plants as well as timber for shipbuilding. The Spanish habit of leaving domestic animals, such as cattle and pigs, to run wild on the various islands had led to an increasing population of feral stock which provide an abundance of meat and hides.

The major obstacle to permanent European settlement of Antigua was the chronic scarcity of water. Laments over the meagerness of the water supply run like a lugubrious refrain throughout Antiguan history, and even today the specter of drought has not been fully exorcised. A map of Antigua dating from the eighteenth century (see p. 9) bears the rueful caption:

> Antigua is a fine Island, tho' it has not one Single Spring of Water in it: So that in—times of drouth when all their Ponds—are dry, and their Cisterns almost empty, they are obliged to fetch their fresh Water from Montserrat, in times of War; or, in times of Peace from that and Guardaloup a Neighbouring French Island.

The notorious scarcity (though not a total lack, as in the mapmaker's hyperbole) of fresh springs is compounded by a very erratic and low rainfall. Yet as we shall see presently, not all of the aridity of Antigua throughout its history is to be attributed to Mother Nature.

Both Spanish and French sent out expeditions to Antigua to explore the possibilities of colonization, but both nations balked at the double menace of Carib raids and shortage of springs. It was the English who doughtily surmounted the human and natural obstacles, when in 1632 they dispatched a party of settlers from the nearby island of St. Kitts under the leadership of Captain Edward Warner.

The location of the pioneer English colony in Antigua was what is now called Carlisle Bay on the southern coast in the vicinity of Old Road Village—a choice determined, not unnaturally, by the presence of a fresh water spring. The first town grew up at Falmouth, near the appropriately named English Harbour, which had a large and sheltered port. Since those days, the English have retained possession of the island in one form or another with the single exception of a brief period in 1666 when it was captured by the rival French. The French presence is nowhere to be discerned today. Not even a sonorous placename remains to register their ephemeral sovereignty.

By contrast, the English presence in Antigua precipitated great changes in the physical and human environment and, more than any other factor, has shaped the physiognomy of the island. With their coming, the axe quite literally descended on the forests and woodlands of Antigua with the thoroughness of a biblical swarm of locusts, and in place of the native forests were planted alien crops and, soon to follow, alien peoples. By 1676 (or less than five decades from the time of original settlement) roughly 70 percent of the total land area of the island had been swallowed up by sugar estates. (Harris, 1965, p. 88) Today, the eerie presence of abandoned sugar mills in the most unlikely spots is testimony to the extensiveness of the earlier cultivation.

But sugar was not always king. The English had first begun by following in the footsteps of the Arawaks and planting a native cultigen, tobacco, for export to the mother country. As the market rapidly became glutted and the soil less productive, they switched to indigo and ginger—both Southeast Asian imports. Sugar, another Asian import, was already beginning to compete with indigo by the 1670's. The decisive step, however, from small-scale cultivation of sugar to the full-fledged plantation system was taken by a shrewd English aristocrat named Christopher Codrington, who in 1674 came to Antigua from Barbados and established a pioneer sugar estate in an area of the limestone district. Codrington called his plantation Betty's Hope, after his daughter. His example was spectacularly successful and was quickly emulated by others, so that by 1700 all of the central plain and the limestone district, as well as portions of the volcanic area, were planted in sugar plantations.

Hand in hand with the proliferation of the plantations went the annihilation of the native vegetation. Most of the forest cover and evergreen woodland was levelled in a manner as thorough as it was irreversible and short-sighted. For the planter's ideal in preparing new land for cultivation was nothing less than *total* clearance, such that, in the words of a contemporary, "there remain not any wood, nor bark, nor leaf, nor so much as the least grass." (Davies, 1666, p. 188 in Harris, p. 88) The violence done to the insular environment in the interest of sugar manufacture and profit had severe repercussions on the climate. Like a boomerang, the axe and the fire returned against the planter to harrow him with the specter of drought and desiccation. The link between the dry weather and the total clearance of the land was perceived by a few thoughtful strangers who arrived on the Antiguan scene from Europe. Thus Thomas Shirley who came to take up duties as governor of the island in 1781 (about a century and a half after colonization) reflected soberly on the causes of desiccation in a letter written upon arrival:

The Planters of this Island have experienced a train of Distressful events, the Cause of which may be attributed to the nakedness of the face of the Country, hardly any trees left standing. The populousness of the island and the equal surface of the Land, induced the proprietors to render every part of it as profitable as they could, by everywhere cutting down the woods.

By this injudicious step, the fruits of the Earth are deprived of those periodical supplies of moisture from rain, which they experience in almost every other Island.

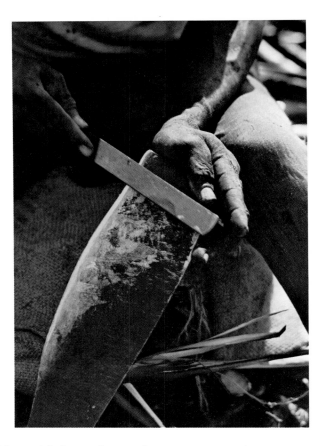

Sharpening the Cutlass

Four or five successive years of dry weather will occur, scorching with heat almost the whole Island, excepting a small chain of mountains, which, from their superior elevation attract the passing clouds. . . . (in Oliver, 1894, Vol. I, p. cxxv)

The appalling human (as opposed to environmental) cost of the plantation system is well known and copiously documented. The Antiguan estate was a microcosm of the New World plantation economy. Black slave labor was, of course, the sine qua non. The English, after using their own paupers and outcasts as indentured servants, and having found the Indians recalcitrant, turned to the west coast of Africa and developed and refined the diabolical machinery of the "triangular trade." By 1678, approximately half of the population of Antigua already consisted of black slaves; the dominant mode of production—the sugar cane plantation—was now firmly installed for centuries to come. The rest of the Antiguan story is fundamentally a footnote to the vicissitudes of sugar.

Eyewitness accounts of plantation slavery in its various phases provide the most graphic picture of life in old Antigua. For a vivid impression of what it was to be a captured African confronting a slave ship bound for the Indies, here is an excerpt from the memoirs of an Ibo ex-slave: *Equiano's Travels: His Autobiography: The Interesting Narrative of the Life of Olaudah Equiano or Gustavus Vassa the African:*

The first object which saluted my eyes when I arrived on the coast was the sea, and a slave ship which was then riding at anchor and waiting for its cargo. These filled me with astonishment, which was soon converted into terror when I was carried on board. I was immediately handled and tossed up to see if I were sound by some of the crew, and I was now persuaded that I had gotten into a world of bad spirits and that they were going to kill me. Their complexions too differing so much from ours, their long hair and the language they spoke (which was very different

from any I had ever heard) united to confirm me in this belief. Indeed such were
the horrors of my views and fears at the moment that, if ten thousand worlds had
been my own, I would have freely parted with them all to have exchanged my
condition with that of the meanest slave in my own country. When I looked round
the ship too and saw a large furnace or copper boiling and a multitude of black
people of every description chained together, every one of their countenances
expressing dejection and sorrow, I no longer doubted of my fate; and quite over-
powered with horror and anguish, I fell motionless on the deck and fainted. When
I recovered a little I found some black people about me, who I believed were some
of those who had brought me on board and had been receiving their pay; they talked
to me in order to cheer me, but all in vain. I asked them if we were not to be eaten
by those white men with horrible looks, red faces, and loose hair. They told me I
was not, and one of the crew brought me a small portion of spirituous liquor in a
wine glass, but being afraid of him I would not take it out of his hand. One of the
blacks therefore took it from him and gave it to me, and I took a little down my
palate, which instead of reviving me, as they thought it would, threw me into the
greatest consternation at the strange feeling it produced, having never tasted such
any liquor before. Soon after this the blacks who brought me on board went off,
and left me abandoned to despair.

I now saw myself deprived of all chance of returning to my native country or even
the least glimpse of hope of gaining the shore, which I now considered as friendly;
and I even wished for my former slavery in preference to my present situation,
which was filled with horrors of every kind, still heightened by my ignorance of
what I was to undergo. I was not long suffered to indulge my grief; I was soon put
down under the decks and there I received such a salutation in my nostrils as I had
never experienced in my life: so that with the loathsomeness of the stench and
crying together, I became so sick and low that I was not able to eat, nor had I the

least desire to taste anything. I now wished for the last friend, death, to relieve me; but soon, to my grief, two of the white men offered me eatables, and on my refusing to eat, one of them held me fast by the hands and laid me across I think the wind-lass, and tied my feet while the other flogged me severely. I had never experienced anything of this kind before, and although, not being used to the water, I naturally feared that element the first time I saw it, yet nevertheless could I have got over the nettings I would have jumped over the side, but I could not; and besides, the crew used to watch us very closely who were not chained down to the decks, lest we should leap into the water: and I have seen some of these poor African prisoners most severely cut for attempting to do so, and hourly whipped for not eating. This indeed was often the case with myself. In a little time after, amongst the poor chained men I found some of my own nation, which in a small degree gave ease to my mind. I inquired of these what was to be done with us; they gave me to under-stand we were to be carried to these white people's country to work for them. I then was a little relieved, and thought if it were no worse than working, my situation was not so desperate; but still I feared I should be put to death, the white people looked and acted, as I thought, in so savage a manner; for I had never seen among my people such instances of brutal cruelty, and this not only shewn towards us blacks but also to some of the whites themselves. One white man in particular I saw, when we were permitted to be on deck, flogged so unmercifully with a large rope near the foremast that he died in consequence of it; and they tossed him over the side as they would have done a brute. This made me fear these people the more, and I expected nothing less than to be treated in the same manner. (Edwards, 1967, pp. 25-27)

What was life like for the black slave who survived the gruesome journey to the New World of the Antilles? Modern historians have labored to reconstruct it as objectively

as possible within the limits of their discipline (as for instance, Elsa Goveia in her exemplary volume: *Slave Society in the British Leeward Islands at the End of the Eighteenth Century*). In the special case of Antigua, we are fortunate in having several contemporary descriptions written by European observers, such as the *Journal of a Lady of Quality*. These are, of course, flawed by the racialist perspectives of the narrators, but read with this caveat in mind, they contain some valuable information presented in a lively manner. Perhaps the most fascinating source for the Antigua scene are the letters written by John Luffman who visited the island colony in the eighteenth century when the plantation system was in full swing. The following extracts from Luffman's precious work, entitled *A Brief Account of the Island of Antigua*, are chosen to provide a kind of mosaic, albeit fragmentary, of the new world created by the Antiguan plantocrats and their backers:

(THE ARRIVAL OF THE SLAVES ON THE ISLAND   *from letter 19*)

Thus are the degraded sons of Africa brought to the West-Indian shores; and they are treated in the following manner on their arrival here, previous to the day of sale: As soon as the anchor is over the vessel's side, and the captain gone on shore to give in his account of the cargo, the slaves are brought upon the deck (having been shaved some days before they made the land), where they are cleansed from the stench and vermin contracted on the passage, and their skins rubbed with oil or grease to give them a sleek appearance. This business being done, they are sent on shore, under the care of some petty officers and seamen, to the merchant to whom the cargo is consigned, who deposits them altogether in an empty store or warehouse, contiguous to the wharfs, when after being advertised for sale, and walked about the town, preceded by a drum beating and flag flying, for the purpose of attracting the attention of the inhabitants to the persons about to be sold; and when the merchant has sent written notices of the time of such sale to the planters or others, whom he thinks likely to become purchasers, the sale is announced by a trumpet sounding, while the ships ensign, or some other flag, is displayed from a window, or from the top of the place where the negroes are deposited; and so eager are the whites to see these ill-fated people, that the doors of

such receptacles are crowded almost as much as those of the theatre, when the immortal Garrick, or the inimitable Siddons were to represent the finest passages from our greatest and most favored poets.

The purchasers of slaves are as particular in examining them before they strike a bargain, as a butcher, at Smithfield market, when dealing for sheep. As soon as bought, they are walked to the respective plantations of their owners, where the hoe is frequently put into hands, hitherto unused to labor, and as soft as the finest lady's in Europe.

These cargoes average from thirty-seven to forty pounds sterling per head.

(LIVING CONDITIONS OF THE SLAVES *from letter 22*)

The common allowance, for the support of a house slave, is three bits per week, and although it appears so very trifling and insufficient, it is generally preferred by them, to being fed from the tables of their masters or mistresses . . .

The weekly allowance of a field negro, is from three to five quarts of horse beans, rice, or Indian corn, with three or four salt herrings, or a piece of salted beef or pork, of about two pounds weight; but when the estates have such provisions as yams, eddas, guinea corn, sweet potatoes, plaintains, and bananas, they are served with them in lieu of the former, and as nearly as possible in the same proportion. In addition to this allowance, every slave on a plantation, whether male or female, when they have attained their 14th or 15th year, has a piece of ground, from twenty five to thirty square feet, allotted to them, which by some is industriously and advantageously cultivated, and by others totally neglected. These patches are found to be of material benefit to the country, their produce principally supplying the Sunday market (which is the greatest throughout the week, from being the negroes holiday) with vegetables. They are also allowed to raise pigs, goats and fowls, and it is by their attention to these articles, that the whites are prevented from starving, during such times of the year as vessels cannot come to these coasts with safety.

The clothing of a field slave consists of a blanket, which serves them not only to sleep upon (tho' some have beds of dried plaintain leaves), but to fasten about their bodies in damp weather, also a piece of woollen cloth, called a babbaw, which goes round the waist, a blue woollen jacket and party colored hat of the same material. Their drink, as per allowance is water. When sick they are attended by young doctors,

whose principals contract with the owners of estates, or their attorney's by the year, and the common price is six shillings currency, equal to three shillings and nine-pence sterling, per head. It is the business of these assistants to visit the estates, thus put under the care of their employers, twice a week, and on every planta-tion is a hospital or sick-house, where the slaves, as soon as infected with disorder, or having received hurt (the latter of which frequently happens in crop time) are sent. These places, at least such as have come within my observation, are as bad as you can well suppose, being not only destitute of almost every convenience, but filthy in the extreme, and the attendants generally such negroes as are nearly superannuated or unfit for active employment. I am much surprised how the medical gentlemen, even in the manner this business is performed, can make it pay the expenses attending thereon, at so small a premium, and indeed, I think it is impossible for them to get the keep of one of their horses out of these undertakings although they should make use of the very cheapest drugs that can be procured, or if even only of medicinal simples, the growth of the island.

(THE DAILY ROUND   *from letter 23*)

   The negroes are turned out at sunrise, and employed in gangs from twenty to sixty, or upwards, under the inspection of white overseers, generally poor Scotch lads, who, by their assiduity and industry, frequently become masters of the plantations, to which they came out as indentured servants: subordinate to these overseers, are drivers, commonly called dog-drivers, who are mostly black or mulatto fellows, of the worst disposition; these men are furnished with whips, which, while on duty, they are obliged, on pain of severe punishment to have with them, and are authorized to flog wherever they see the least relaxation from labor; nor is it a consideration with them, whether it proceeds from idleness or inability, paying, at the same time, little or no regard to age or sex. At twelve they are turned in (that is, leave off work) to get what they can to refresh nature with; at half past one the bell rings, when they turn out and resume their labor until sunset; for the last hour they are chiefly employed in picking grass for the cattle, belonging to the estate, and when a sufficiency is collected for that purpose, they gather what they can for themselves, pack it up in bundles, which they carry to Saint John's, on their heads, and sell for one or more dogs [sic], according to the quantity or demand for it.

(MAINTAINING LAW AND ORDER   *from letter 24*)

The punishments inflicted on slaves, in this island, are various and tormenting. The picket, is the most severe, but as its consequences are well known in Europe, particularly among the military, I shall speak no further upon it, than to say it is seldom made use of here, but many other cruelties equally destructive to life, though slower in their operations, are practised by the unfeeling, among which is the thumb-screw, a barbarous invention to fasten the thumbs together, which appears to cause excruciating pain. The iron necklace, is a ring, locked or rivetted about the neck; to these collars are frequently added what are here termed pot-hooks, additions, resembling the hooks or handles of a porridge pot, fixed perpendicularly, the bent or hooked parts turning outwards, which prevents the wearers from laying down their heads with any degree of comfort. The boots are strong iron rings, full four inches in circumference, closed just above the ancles, to these some owners prefix a chain, which the miserable sufferers, if able to work, must manage as well as they can, and it is not unfrequent to see in the streets of this town, at mid-day, negroes chained together by these necklaces as well as by the boots, when let out of their dungeon for a short time to breathe the fresh air, whose crime has been endeavoring to gain that liberty by running away, which they well knew could never be otherwise obtained from their owners. The spurs are rings of iron, similar to the boots, to which are added spikes from three to four inches long, placed horizontally. A chain fastened about the body with a pad-lock, is another mode of tormenting these oppressed race of beings. A boy who has not yet seen his fourteenth year, passes by my house several times in a day, and has done so for these six months past, with no other cloathing; he also lays upon his chains, and although they are as much in point of weight as he ought reasonably to carry, yet he is obliged, through the day to fetch water from the country pond, at the distance of half a mile from the house of his mistress, who is an old widow-woman. To the chains thus put on, a fifty pounds weight is sometimes added as an appendage; this is undoubtedly a prudent measure, and admirably well calculated to keep the slave at home, as it must of course prevent the object thus secured, from escaping the rigor of his destiny. The bilboes, severe floggings, and sundry other methods of torturing these unhappy people, as best suits the caprice or inventive cruelty of their owners or employers, are here inflicted. The public whipper is a white man, who executes his office by a negroe deputy, and the price for every flogging is two bits. (in Oliver, 1894, pp. cxxx-cxxxviii)

Luffman's first-hand descriptions of life on Antiguan plantations dramatize the physical constraints under which the transplanted Africans had to survive and grow. The spiritual parameters of this harrowing existence, however, can never be accurately recreated, despite the tantalizing glimpses we get from ex-slave autobiographies. For an Antiguan of today, trying to come to terms with that experience, so as to interpret the lines in the faces of his contemporaries, it is virtually impossible to translate indignation into meaningful sequences of words. Perhaps it is the unique task of the West Indian poet to do what discursive prose essays cannot do—to remain both lucid and true to the complex memory of the event. Edward Brathwaite—one of the finest poets to emerge in the English-speaking Caribbean—has spoken incisively of the psychological inheritance of plantation slavery in his masterpiece, *Islands,* from which these lines are excerpted:

So looking through a map
of the islands, you see
rocks, history's hot
lies, rot-
ting hulls, cannon
wheels, the sun's
slums: if you hate
us. Jewels,
if there is delight
in your eyes.
The light
shimmers on water,
the cunning
coral keeps it
blue.

Looking through a map
of the Antilles, you see how time
has trapped
its humble servants here. Descendants of the slave do not
lie in the lap
of the more fortunate
gods. The rat
in the warehouse is as much king
as the sugar he plunders.
But if your eyes
are kinder, you will observe
butterflies

how they fly higher
and higher before their hope dries
with endeavour
and they fall among flies.

Looking through a map
of the islands, you see
that history teaches
that when hope
splinters, when the pieces
of broken glass lie
in the sunlight,
when only lust rules
the night, when the dust
is not swept out
of the houses,
when men make noises
louder than the sea's
voices; then the rope
will never unravel
its knots, the branding
iron's travelling flame that teaches
us pain, will never be
extinguished. The island's jewels:
Saba, Barbuda, dry flat-
tened Antigua, will remain rocks,
dots, in the sky-blue frame
of the map.

English Harbour Antigua

PLANTING THE SUGAR-CANE

Eighteen inches of the summit of the Cane is called the top, and used as fodder, the next twelve inches is the most advantageous part for planting; it is separated while gathering in the harvest, and requires particular treatment.

Shortly after having been cut, the plants are placed in water for about twenty-four hours, which is found to assist the budding. If the land be not sufficiently moist to receive the plants, they are tied in small bundles placed perpendicularly, covered with trash, or dried leaves of the Cane, and watered three or four times a day to preserve them. Rain is highly essential to the growth of the young Cane; in drought the plant cannot be committed to the earth with hope of success. When the weather fortunately favours the process of planting, the bundles are conveyed to the piece. The younger Negroes distribute two or three

plants into each Cane-hole, while the most experienced Negroes open cavities in the holes about six inches deep, place the plants horizontally, so that the buds may appear on either side, and cover them. This process requires great attention on the part of the Negroes who are thus intrusted.

The Drivers are trust-worthy persons, and their judgment is on these occasions particularly useful.

The Manager attends the field occasionally, the Overseers being employed in the boiling-house, or the distillery.

This view is taken upon Bodkin's Estate, looking southward.

Monk's Hill, a military station, appears in the back-ground, where signals are hoisted communicating with St. John's.

CUTTING THE SUGAR-CANE

The Sugar-Cane requires between eleven and twelve months to ripen. To assist the judgment in determining when a Cane-piece is sufficiently ripe, a portion of juice is sometimes expressed from a Cane which shall appear a fair specimen of the whole piece, and exposed to the sun for the aqueous parts to evaporate; if the crystallization be evident to the touch, and retain firmness, the Cane-piece may be considered fit for harvest.

The Negroes, provided with cutting bills, then arrange themselves as when hoeing, each taking his or her respective row. The upper part of the Cane, comprising plant and top, is first cut off, the plant is separated, and the Cane is then divided into junks of about three feet in length, cutting close to the earth. The green top is used to bind the junks into bundles of twenty or thirty each. The cutters strip the trash from the Cane as they proceed, and move it from one to another, till it is collected in swaths about twenty feet apart; this is done that the junks of Cane may be unincumbered in the intervals, while being bound by the inferior gang.

The trash is afterwards collected as fuel, and the green tops as fodder for the cattle.

The Manager, during this busy time, is employed in arranging the required supply for the Mill, which in a good breeze demands the greatest exertion of every one on the estate. It may be proper to observe, that when the Cane plant bears a second or third crop, the Canes are then denominated, first rattoons—second rattoons, &c.

This view is taken upon Delaps' Estate, looking southward.

54

THE MILL YARD

The bundles of Cane are carted and deposited as near as possible to the Mill, to lessen the labour of the Negro-girls, who convey them on their heads to the mill-door, where the junks are placed on a receiving board, and the tops which bound them drawn away for the convenience of the Negro whose duty it is to feed the Mill.

In high winds, two, and sometimes three, feeders are required to supply the cylinders.

The lower works of a Sugar-mill consist of three cylinders placed perpendicularly; that in the centre, being acted upon by the works above, causes the cylinders on the sides to revolve by means of corresponding cogs. The Canes are entered on one side of the centre cylinder, and forced out on the other by means of a *dumb-turner*, which is a simple machine of semicircular form wedged up to the cylinder, so as to force the pressed Canes out by the revolving of the works. The expressed juice is received into a leaden channel beneath the cylinders, and drains into a reservoir on one side of the Mill, where, passing through two wooden strainers, it is cleansed from particles of Cane, and runs along a metal tube to the boiling-house.

The *Magos* or bruised refuse of the Cane, returned by the dumb-turner, glides down an inclined plane through an aperture in the Mill-wall, whence it is conveyed away upon wooden frames by women, and the old Negroes, spread and turn it in the sun to be afterwards used for fuel.

The Mill is that situated at Gambles, and the accessaries are taken from other estates, to bring them under one point of view, to represent the Mill-yard.

THE BOILING-HOUSE

The juice of the Cane being conveyed by pipes to the boiling-house, is, as occasion may require, received into the simmering coppers, some of which will contain six hundred gallons. In these huge receptacles the juice is made to simmer by a judicious application of heat; during which the due quantity of lime is incorporated, and the greater portion of the impurities brought to the surface. The juice being then drawn off from beneath the scum into the next copper, called a *Clarifier*, is boiled and skimmed until transparent. It is then distributed among the four adjoining coppers called *Taches*, each being kept full, boiled, duly skimmed, and ladled forward till it has, in succession, reached the first Tache, under which the principal fire is placed, extending by a flue to the other three Taches. During this process the evaporation is very great, and the juice acquires particular denominations. In the fourth Tache, that nearest the Clarifier, it is little more than hot juice; in the third, *Liquor*; in the second, *Sirup*; in the first, *Sling*—where it becomes sugar, though in a liquid state. The fire is stopped, the sugar is then ladled into a spout which conducts it to a cooler, where it is lightly agitated on its surface with a kind of spatula, three or four times, till the whole mass is crystallized; the same process being observed upon every fresh surface, or strike, of sugar, received into the coolers. The scum is poured into a gutter extending along the front of the coppers, whence it passes into the distillery. The wind which blows with little variation between N.E. and S.E. enters at the windows, cools the sugar, and expels the steam through the apertures in the roof.

This scene is the Boiling-House upon Delaps' Estate.

CARTING AND PUTTING SUGAR-HOGSHEADS ON BOARD

The want of wharfs on the shores of the Island, has rendered it necessary to resort to an awkward and hazardous method of getting sugars on board.

The small vessels used to convey the Hogsheads to the shipping in the harbour of St. John's, or English harbour, are called Drogers, of from twenty to thirty tons burthen, having boats provided with timbers on which the Hogshead may rest.

The boats are brought to the proper depth of water, and are forced down on one side; two spars or skids are then extended from the gunwales to the shore, on which the hogsheads are rolled into the boat, at the recoil of the wave: much dexterity is necessary to ac-

complish this without shipping water with the sugar.

Many estates, remotely situated from places of shipment, are provided with store-houses upon the beach, in which Sugar and Rum are occasionally deposited, in readiness to be received on board the small craft, to be forwarded to the King's Beam, at St. John's, where the duty is ascertained: the Sugar is then shipped for England, a voyage of uncertain duration, usually made in four weeks; but too often occupying two months, from the Captains being compelled to cross the Atlantic under the disadvantages of varying winds.

This scene is in Willoughby Bay.

59

View near St. John's Antigua

OFFSHOOTS

The story of emancipation and its aftermath is often recounted from the point of view of the metropolitan scene, with the main focus on the humanitarian propagandists in England and their valiant parliamentary struggles. But what of pressures from within the slave population? Did the Antiguan blacks, for instance, remain passive within their insular prison of 108 square miles?

By no means. Resistance and rebellion were not exclusive to the larger islands such as Jamaica and Haiti, where large mountains offered secure hiding-places for runaways like the Maroons. Slave uprisings did occur in Antigua, as elsewhere in the Antilles, throughout the eighteenth century, shaking, like sudden earthquakes, the formidable pyramid at its very base. The most powerful tremor took place in the year 1736 and is known in the official literature as the "Antiguan conspiracy." We can document the uprising from the Calendar of State Papers for the year 1736, in which local governors and plantocrats registered their fears in epistolary narratives marked by a mixture of fact, rumor and fantasy:

Antigua, 30 December 1736. Report to Governor Mathew of an enquiry into the negro conspiracy. The slaves chiefly concerned were those born on the Gold Coast whom we style coromantees, led by Court a slave of Thomas Kerby; and those born in the colonies whom we call creoles, led by Tomboy a master carpenter belonging to Thomas Hanson. Court, we are told, was of a considerable family in his own country, brought here at ten years of age, and covertly assumed among his countrymen here the title of king. Both men were well-treated by their masters, Tomboy being allowed to take negro apprentices and make all the profits he could. The other principals were Hercules, Jack, Scipio, Ned, Fortune and Toney, all creoles except Fortune who was either a creole or brought here as an infant. The most active incendiaries under Court and Tomboy were Secundi and Jacko, both creoles of French parentage and both initiated into the Roman Catholic religion. Their employments were crafts, overseeing and house-service. When and by whom the design was first begun cannot be certainly fixed; probably it was by Court, and we know that it was in agitation about November 1735. The chief measures taken to corrupt our slaves were entertainments of dancing and feasting under colour of innocent pretences; those corrupted were bound by oaths. A new government was to be established when the whites were extirpated: Court was flattered by all with being king, but the creoles had privately resolved to settle a commonwealth and make slaves of the coromantees. . . .

The method first proposed for executing the plot was that Tomboy should procure the making of the seats for a great ball to be held on 11 October last, at which all the people of note in the island would be present. He was to contrive laying gunpowder in the house to be fired when the dancing was in progress. Three or four parties of 300-400 slaves were to enter the town and put the whites to the sword; the forts and shipping in the harbour were to be seized. The ball, however, was put off to 30 October, whereupon some conspirators wished to act immediately; but Court persuaded them to defer the action till then. Signs were not wanting of the impending danger, and these led the governor to order an enquiry which led to the discovery of the plot, much owing to the confessions of the various slaves. On the evidence of the facts discovered, the first twelve of the conspirators in the annexed list were executed. Further examination, however, caused us to see that much remained to be done; by various evidences, 35 more slaves were executed and 42 more, the evidence against them being less full, are recommended for banishment. All those executed or recommended for banishment are known to have taken the oath; this was by drinking a health in liquor with gravedirt and sometimes cock's blood infused, and sometimes the person swearing laid his hand on a live cock. The general tenor of the oath was to kill the whites. The execution of the first twelve did not break the conspiracy, for at least 50 took the oath on 26 October last after the executions.

We may say with certainty that the particular inducement to the slaves to set this plot on foot, next to the hope of freedom, was the inequality of numbers of white and black. We think gentlemen should reside on their estates; that men of the best figure and fortune should not put slights on the commissions of peace and militia; that slaves should not become craftsmen, overseers or tradesmen; that more of our menial servants should be white; and that no fiddlers for gain, except white, should be suffered. The presence of the King's troops was heartening to us and

intimidating to the slaves; we could do with more. A person called Mulatto Jack
was brought before us as a criminal slave concerned in the plot: but he alleged
that he was free born in Ireland and stolen thence and sold here as a slave. We
think he proved his allegation, and we submit it to the legislature whether this
mitigates his crime. A free negro named John Coteen and a free mulatto called Tom
were likewise charged before us. Jack and Coteen, were slaves' evidence admitted,
are undoubtedly guilty; but the evidence against Tom is not strong. As it is not in our
power to try free persons we submit their cases to the legislature. We propose that the
slaves who made the discovery should be rewarded: this will help to make them
more distrustful of one another. . . .

As this horrid conspiracy cannot but be heard of wherever people hold corre-
spondence with Antigua, it will no doubt be variously animadverted upon; and as
slavery is the very odium of the Englishmen some of our countrymen may do
it to our disadvantage. Yet slavery is among us not of choice but of necessity, and
unless (as it is not to be imagined) our mother-country should quit the trade of the
sugar-colonies Englishmen must continue to be masters of their slaves. There
were two steps in particular taken by us in our enquiry which might have been
excepted to. First, trying the criminals privately and excluding all whites except
the constables, and twice or thrice whites who were not masters of slaves. We
found our proceedings much retarded by whites asking questions, especially the
masters of slaves under examination. Secrecy was necessary to prevent the flight
of those on whom suspicion might fall. Secondly, admitting slaves to be witnesses
after conviction of what we termed a treasonable conspiracy. There is little weight
in this. A slave is not a person known by the laws of England, and in the eye of our
laws is the same person after conviction as before, being incapable of giving evidence
except against each other. Slaves can lose no credit nor have their blood corrupted
nor forfeit property nor suffer disability by attainder. By an act of this island it is
expressly left to the discretion of the justices to examine the slaves as witnesses
and give what credit to his testimony they think it deserves. We always made
considerable allowances for the hopes and fears of those under conviction, and we
have leaned more to the merciful than the severe. An Act being passed for inflicting

torture on persons suspected of the plot, we three times made fruitless experiment thereof, and then declined further use. (K. G. Davies, 1963, pp. 11-13)

In the insecure aftermath of the same "conspiracy," an Antiguan planter, John Yeamans, the proud owner of an estate that still bears his name, made the following petition to the King:

Petition of John Yeamans, agent for Antigua, and of the planters and merchants whose names are subscribed, to the King. The negroes of Antigua have for some time past been contriving and had nearly executed a most cruel and execrable plot. By the providence of God and the vigilance of the civil magistrate the said plot has been discovered: the governor and principal families were to have been blown up with gunpowder on 30 October last, and from this a signal taken for all negroes to rise and cut off every white person, to which they bound themselves by horrid oaths. The chief conspirators were natives of this island employed in houses or bred to trades. There are at least 24,000 negroes in the island and not above 3,000 whites. The inhabitants continue under the most terrible apprehensions of further attempts. The regular soldiers consist of five companies of 31 men each, much too small a force for security. The militia has been continuously under arms since the discovery of the plot to the great detriment of business. A like conspiracy was discovered in the island about eight years ago, but petitioners find that the punishments then inflicted were not sufficient to deter a second attempt. They therefore pray for augmentation of the forces in the Leeward Islands. (K. G. Davies, 1963, p. 50)

Despite such rumblings as these, the only West Indian island, large or small, whose slaves succeeded in liberating themselves from the yoke of slavery was Haiti (or Saint Domingue as it was formerly called). The gory tale of the only successful slave revolt in history has been graphically retold by the West Indian author C. L. R. James in his book, *Black Jacobins*. But in Antigua as in the rest of the Antilles, evolutionary change, punctuated by sporadic uprisings, led instead to emancipation and its contradictions. Whether as a result of revolutionary or evolutionary

changes, the seeds of liberation were sown by the very dynamics of the slave system itself—a system which demanded a disproportionately large ratio of slaves to masters. The movement toward freedom was directly related to the scope and pace of the transplantation.

Though the violent uprooting of blacks from the West African homeland and their transfer to the Caribbean islands was accompanied by untold human losses (both in the course of the Middle Passage and on the insular colonies themselves), still the cargoes of slaves poured in from across the Atlantic into the apparently bottomless pit of the sugar industry with its insatiable demand for cheap labor. From virtually the very beginning, the slave population heavily outnumbered the white planter class; by the end of the eighteenth century there were, in the Leeward Islands, 83,000 blacks, nearly 3,000 free people of color, and 8,400 whites. Slave society had assumed the rigid shape of a layered pyramid, with each layer kept separate, insofar as this was humanly possible, by the slave laws.

In the boom conditions of the late eighteenth century, conspicuous consumption was the order of the day both for the absentee English landowners and their local representatives. But the fabulous monoculture of sugar was doomed to decline, bowing, like a reluctant tree in a hurricane, to myriad pressures from without and within— among the former the interruption of direct trade with the mainland occasioned by the American War of Independence. Slaves, in the meantime, had become more and more expensive to purchase and to maintain. Few planters, it seems, had followed the ingenious policy of Codrington, who set up a breeding ground for slaves in the island of Barbuda as a means of supplying his Antigua plantations!

The economic crisis coincided with the birth of the anti-slavery movement, launched by humanitarian groups in the mother country. This is not the place to expatiate on the complex causes of that movement; historians continue the inquiry and debate. One or two of the more salient ironies, however, deserve to be recounted.

The very same planters who had hysterically fought the humanitarians under the conviction that freedom for the slaves would spell financial ruin for themselves were soon to discover that it meant, on the contrary, economic revival for their flagging industry. In retrospect, the specter of freedom turned out, from the planters'

(text continued on page 86)

perspective, to be no specter at all. The author of *Antigua and the Antiguans*, writing only a decade after emancipation was proclaimed in 1834, could affirm on the basis of her personal observation in the island:

> After dwelling so long upon the gloomy subject of slavery, it is pleasing to turn to the more cheering prospects of the country under a system of perfect freedom.
>
> It must be allowed that, for a few years previous to emancipation, the Antiguan planters were in a state of great perturbation. They plainly perceived, from the state of affairs, that the thraldom of slavery must be broken— that Britain would no longer allow her children to traffic openly in flesh and blood; and, finally, that they must, whether with a good grace or sullen deportment, give up their right to slaves. Still the change from slavery to freedom was a great revolution, a mighty crisis; and urgent and inevitable as it was, who could tell what would be its results. From this cause, property in Antigua diminished, for some few years, greatly in value; and many estates might have been then purchased for a comparative trifle.
>
> But this depression did not continue long, for no sooner was the deed done, and the chain which bound the negro to his fellow-man irrecoverably snapped asunder, than it was found, even by the most sceptical, that free-labour was decidedly more advantageous to the planter than the old system of slavery. That, in fact, an estate could be worked for less by free labour than it could when so many slaves— including old and young, weak and strong—were obliged to be maintained by the proprietors. . . .
>
> In days of slavery it required an immense capital to establish a sugar plantation, as well as a large annual expenditure to carry on the affairs of the estate when established. Perhaps a sugar estate had a gang of two hundred slaves upon it, yet out of this large number possibly there might not be more than

sixty or seventy efficient negroes, the surplus being composed of helpless old men and women, children and infants, and emaciated and cureless invalids. Still law obliged the owner to feed, clothe, house, and procure medical attendance for the entire number; and little as their allowance was, yet, in dry seasons in particular, when the crops of yams and other island provisions failed, the maintenance of so many persons was attended with great expense, while at the same time, perhaps, not more than one-third the number were of any use in agricultural employments.

Under the free system, this tie upon the planter is entirely annulled; for he now employs but a sufficient number of labourers to carry on the estate-work, and the negroes support themselves, as well as their old people and children, out of their weekly earnings and the privileges which they still enjoy upon the properties where they are domiciled.   (Flannigan, 1844, Vol. II, pp. 155-158)

For the majority of the ex-slaves in the small islands of the Leewards, emancipation signalled an important change in legal status only. With no economic alternatives in sight to the plantation system, they returned immediately and without euphoria to the cane fields of their former masters, there to eke out a living under austere conditions. A more poignant illustration of these words from Ecclesiastes it would be hard to imagine:

What profit hath a man of all his labour which he taketh under the sun? One generation passeth away, and another generation cometh: but the earth abideth forever. . . . All things are full of labour; man cannot utter it: the eye is not satisfied with seeing, nor the ear filled with hearing. The thing that hath been, it is that which shall be; and that which is done is that which shall be done: and there is no new thing under the sun. . . .

The Reverend George A. Weston

ANTIGUA
PRIDE

We began our opening discussion of aspects of Antigua's past from the fortified summit of Shirley Heights. Mingling with the alien fauna—the nibbling goats and the scuttling mongooses—we were in a position to observe the physical vestiges of a violence that dispossessed the aborigines and converted a wooded ridge into a dry, cactus-covered height.

Shirley Heights is an extreme case of the ecological degradation that typifies the Antiguan landscape today. The assault on the native flora that began quietly with Arawak fires and reached a crescendo with the planter's axe has been steadily carried forward by charcoal-burners and browsing flocks of goats. As in the Greek islands, the goat, prized for its meat at Antiguan village banquets of "kiddie stew," plays untold havoc with the land, and quickens the pace of erosion. Among plants, an introduced species, the acacia (or "cossie" as it is locally known) everywhere asserts its hardihood and indestructibility among a sea of other aliens. No less indestructible are the Antiguan people: descendants of the African slaves who were captured in the Old World and eventually released from limbo to make a living among the hills and valleys of the Limestone Caribbees.

During the slave days, portions of arable land adjacent to plantations were set aside for cultivation by the slaves. Known as "provision grounds," they supported extra subsistence crops for the overworked laborers. After emancipation, the ex-slaves were often forced to expend their efforts at horticulture on marginal and ecologically unsuitable lands. In some cases, new villages were founded in low-lying areas peripheral to estates, and given proud titles that proclaimed the "free" status of the inhabitants—hence Liberta and Freetown.

Many of the crops that Antiguan blacks successfully grew, and continue to grow, on their small plots, were originally brought over from Africa in the holds of slave ships. Such staples as eddoes, okras, yams and eggplant (anchoba), formed part of the regular cargo on the Middle Passage. Familiar Antiguan dishes, like the delicious "pepperpot" (once described by the Englishman, Bryan Edwards, in the early nineteenth century as an "exceedingly palatable and wholesome mess") originated as a meal served up by ingenious peasant women to their husbands laboring on the plantations.

Other dishes which remain popular even today seem to have originated in the economic demands of the slave system. The mainstay of Antiguan cuisine, *funjee,* probably owes its origin to the early importation of foodstuffs from North America to feed the slave population. The ingredients of funjee (which is made from cornmeal and is often served with dried or fresh fish) can readily be seen in a bill of lading from a typical cargo brought into the Leeward Islands in the seventeenth century, e.g., the following partial listing which is dated 2 October 1688:

1	Barrell of onions
9	hogsheads of Bass fish
21	hogsheads of Cod fish
18	hogsheads of Scale ditto
27	Halfe barrells of Pork
10	Barrells of Mackrell
2	Barrells of Pickled Codfish
700	foot of boards
9000	of shingles
4	Tierces of Indian corn
1000	weight of bread
7000	hogshead staves

(Higham, 1921, p. 257)

As a supplement to these staples of diet, fruits like the mango and breadfruit were introduced from Southeast Asia by the colonizers and soon spread like multiplying goats in their new habitat. Nowadays, the mango with its luscious yellow fruit is so common, even on remote slopes, that it is difficult for many Antiguans to accept the fact that it is a relatively late import.

Seafood remains the main dietary link with the Amerindian past. The ingenious Arawak method of stalking fish among the reefs, with the fisherman's head submerged with the aid of calabash gourds, has given way to the more conventional hooks, lines, and nets. Antiguan fishermen, though greatly reduced in number, continue to supply the islanders with the fruits of the subtropical sea, and Antiguan women continue to cook on coal-pots their highly seasoned bowls of fried, stewed, or boiled fish.

The growth of small-scale peasant agriculture in the Caribbean islands is a testament to the resourcefulness of a people under adverse conditions. In the outer Leewards, with their capricious rainfall and impoverished soils, it is nothing short of the miraculous. Yet as remarkable as this achievement may be, it should not be imagined that the Antiguan "peasant" woman in the classic picture postcard, her head laden with a basket of provisions as she plods to market, is in any way to be regarded as a figure of romance. The unpalatable facts of West Indian history do not permit the sentimentalizing of the relation of peasant to his ancestral plot. The Antiguan ex-slave and his descendants working in the field, is, and sees himself, much more as a laborer, a kind of rural proletarian, than a "peasant" with all the pseudo-autonomy that the term sometimes connotes in the Old World. Today the internal market generated by the Antiguan peasants is threatened with extinction as imported foodstuffs flood the new supermarkets of St. John's. Frozen okra, imported from the storehouses of American agribusiness, now competes with the meager local specimens, coaxed out of a recalcitrant soil in decades of drought.

Where does Antiguan agriculture stand today? Attempts at diversification are made from time to time, but the monoculture of sugar still bestrides and controls the island. Specialized commodities such as the famous sea-island cotton and the pineapple have provided alternatives to king sugar, but the fortunes of these minor dynasties have fluctuated widely. The case of the pineapple is spectacular and representative.

So flourishing was the pineapple in Antigua in former times that the fruit was adopted as the official emblem of the island. Today the pineapple is seldom grown for export except in a few recently established government plots. Even so, the diminutive and aromatic Antiguan pineapple has long enjoyed a deserved reputation among connoisseurs as the nonpareil of pineapples. One variety especially— the inimitable Antigua Black—flourishes only in certain restricted areas of the island.

From all accounts, it appears that the pineapple was known to, and cherished by, the Arawaks. The European settlers soon learned to cultivate it both for its taste and for the supposedly medicinal properties of its juice, as is evident in the following quote from a seventeenth century observer, John Davies:

> In Physick the Vertues of it are these: The juice does admirably recreate and exhilarate the Spirits, and comfort the Heart; it also fortifies the Stomack, cureth Queasiness, and causeth Appetite: it gives present ease to such as are troubled with the Stone, or stoppage of Urine; nay it destroys the force of Poyson . . .
>
> (Davies, 1666, p. 59)

John Luffman in his *Brief Account* alludes to the unique savor of the celebrated Antigua Black variety: "The pines of the island are superior to all others, both in size and taste, there are two sorts, the yellow and the black, equally grateful, and in the proper seasons, as many may be bought for two or three shillings sterling as would fill a bushel." (Luffman in Oliver, 1894, vol. I, p. cxxii) The subsequent tale of the decline of the Antiguan pineapple industry is another illustration of the evils of the sugar monoculture when carried to excess. Perhaps the revival of the Antigua Black will one day accompany the general resurgence of native agriculture which the island desperately needs if it is to stave off the overwhelming pressures of neocolonialism.

In the interim, the Antiguan economy, still chained to sugar, lies moribund. As the sugar cane industry slowly expires and peasants desert the unproductive land, thousands of unemployed Antiguans emigrate to England to seek jobs in the factories of Birmingham and other industrial centers. By one of those ironies which belong to West Indian history, the British slave trade has brought a kind of belated retribution in the immigrant black population of England, reversing one phase of the transatlantic journey. As Mother England closes her doors, the new black diaspora from the islands continues to search for outlets which are becoming more and more scarce. The transplanted Africans are once again being uprooted, as the pressures of people on the resources of a small island increase like the growth chart of a tropical depression which becomes first a storm and then a full-blown hurricane.

For those who remain, the prospects of autonomy in the economic (rather than the political) sense are dim. The tourist trade—now being touted as the panacea of Antigua's ills—promises, if its present structure is maintained, to enrich a few foreign entrepreneurs while generating a few jobs. But from the point of view of the historical experience of the Antiguan people, the transfer from the cane field to the hotel lobby merely represents the return of colonialism in a different dress.

Despite these grave socioeconomic verities, Antiguan culture somehow maintains its vitality. This resilient culture is, of course, a curious amalgam of African and European elements, but genuine creativity, wherever it finds artistic expression, is largely the outcome of the African ingredient in our heritage.

How does the African presence manifest itself in the style of Antiguan culture? The most striking manifestation is in the language. Individual words of African origin like *nyam* (meaning "to eat") appear in the Antiguan vocabulary, but the most significant retentions are in the grammatical structure and tonal qualities of the vernacular. Verbal art in the form of folktales, proverbs and calypsos, constitutes an important sphere of survival for West African culture traits, despite the heterogeneity of the slaves' origin. Thus Anansi, the trickster spider of Antiguan folktale, is none other than the Ashanti folk hero of the same name transferred to a Caribbean environment.

Outside of the linguistic arena and oral traditions, the most conspicuous instance of transmission in Antigua is the persistent popularity of the game of *wari*—a complicated arithmetical game played with seeds and parallel holes on a rectangular wooden board. Widely distributed with minor variations throughout Western Africa, wari is played by young and old with zeal and immense skill all over Antigua: in villages and in the town, on sidewalks, in roadside rum shops and in backyards.

Other survivals are more subtle and controversial. Ways of walking or of resting, dancing and singing, gesticulating and "chupsing," are notoriously difficult to describe to anyone's satisfaction. Yet the indisputable fact remains that a West Indian responding to African highlife music immediately senses its affinity to calypso and somehow knows that the Antiguan iron-band at Carnival with its polyrhythmic percussions is the descendant of the African drum.

The problem for Antiguan culture today may be simply phrased: how do we come to terms with the African past? The paradox of our cultural situation is that while things African are officially stigmatized as backward and attacked, like so many weeds, by the educational system, they persist in forms that are indestructible and life-sustaining.

Some extraordinary members of the older generation sought, albeit in an atavistic way, to bestow status on the African heritage by adhering to the pride-instilling myths of the Garvey movement. Men like the late George A. Weston labored to found elementary schools in Antigua which would invert the traditional values assigned to slave and master and restore a dignity to the African past. The younger Antiguans are seeking to recover a positive identity amidst the imported cultural forms of the Antilles. A strongly rooted identity for our people must, however, await the advent of deep, socioeconomic transformations. Only then, perhaps, will the Antiguans be able to confront the African presence without ambivalence, at last refusing to romanticize it while accepting its fructifying influence.

———◂•▸———

Rural Antigua—the main focus of this book—is by no means the complete picture of the Antiguan cosmos. The motor car, not the donkey, is the chief mode of transportation in the capital, St. John's, and increasingly in the countryside as well. Here and there, telephone poles compete with flamboyants and palms for pride of place and a desalinization plant is rendering obsolete the old home-made barrel cistern. In the town, supermarkets, their shelves stocked with frozen meats and vegetables imported from abroad, are displacing the local market for many members of the population. On all sides, the coastline is being transformed; the splendid coves on the leeward side where the flamingoes once poised their fragile legs are now dotted with luxury hotels, or yield their virgin sands to the cement mixer.

Political, as distinct from economic, power is in the hands of the Antiguans themselves. We govern ourselves according to a formula of "statehood in association" [with Britain] which is one step removed from full independence. Attempts at federation—the consolidation of all former British islands into a larger political entity—have failed conspicuously. There is much residual talk of unity and cooperation, but each island remains fundamentally unto itself. The larger islands, like Jamaica and Trinidad, which have natural resources such as bauxite and oil, pursue their own ways of industrialization; the smaller, like Antigua and St. Kitts, cling to an obsolete and bankrupt monoculture or venture into the dubious arena of tourism.

Despite the glamor of tourism, the social and economic conditions imposed by the moribund sugar industry persist and will persist until rural Antigua again becomes the focus of our attention and efforts. As the doors of emigration close one by one in their faces, the Antiguans "from country"—by far the majority—must be granted at least the means to self-sufficiency, so that they can step out of the vicious circle that leads from sugar cane field to hotel lobby.

Antigua Pride is a tough, resilient, erect plant, yet it flourishes only on dry slopes and among persistent ruins. Antigua Black is the nonpareil among pineapples, but it cannot thrive without intense affection and awareness of its true value. Anansi—the spider-hero of our folklore—is the cleverest creature on earth and can outsmart even the powerful lion, but ultimately he will have to build new and stronger webs. As the poet Edward Brathwaite succinctly puts it:

> For the land has lost the memory of the most secret places.
> We see the moon but cannot remember its meaning.
> A dark skin is a chain but it cannot recall the name
> of its tribe. There are no chiefs in the village.
> The gods have been forgotten or hidden.
> A prayer poured on the ground with water,
> with rum, will not bid them to come
> back. Creation has burned to a spider.
> It peeps over the hills with the sunrise
> but prefers to spin webs in the trees.
> The sea is a divider. It is not a life-giver,
> Time's river. The islands are the humped
> backs of mountains, green turtles
> that cannot find their way. Volcanoes
> are voiceless. They have shut their red eyes
> to the weather. The sun that was once a doom of gold to the Arawaks
> is now a flat boom in the sky.

from Islands

Game of Wari

Carrying Home Mangoes

Abandoned Sugar Mill

Afterword

In the summer of 1967 Gregson took me to his home in Antigua for the first time. I had been making photographs seriously for about a year, but in the course of that initial visit my first really significant images began to emerge. I don't think any experience in my work to date has been as exciting as the first confrontation. It was a subject which electrified my whole being: the palms, the sea, the clouds in the late afternoon sky, the wooden huts and tin fences, the animals, the lively children, and the light!—You have to know the tropics to know that light.

After our marriage in 1968, Gregson and I returned to Antigua. And returned every summer thereafter. The photographs kept emerging with the seasons, and with each season they reflected my development as a photographer and as an adopted Antiguan. I am aware of the possible distortions and misinterpretations which can so easily develop from the preconceptions of a foreigner making pictures in an alien culture, but I made every attempt to recognize my own cultural projections and to present Antiguans in the most straightforward way possible. As my knowledge about Antigua's history and culture grew, my eye became more aware and, I hope, my seeing more penetrating. Since it has never been my intention to catalogue all aspects of Antiguan life, I have tried, through the careful selection of certain images, to express a part of what I feel about Antiguan dignity and pride.

Something should be said of the evolution of the concept for *Antigua Black*. In May of 1972 the Reverend George A. Weston died in New York City. He was flown to Antigua and buried in his native land. The Reverend was a very dear friend of ours and a godfather to our daughter, Anika. He used to sit with Gregson and me on those warm evenings when only the music of crickets filled the air. There, on the front porch of the Davis home on Tanner Street, we would listen to George A. tell us stories about his early life in the West Indies and tales of his work with Marcus Garvey. The Reverend Mr. Weston had an incredible memory, and great skill as a raconteur. Often he would begin a story by saying, "You don't know your own history!" and would go on to tell us what he knew of the black man's legacy in Antigua. We had his dictum in mind when we put together *Antigua Black*.

Then, late in 1970, I first saw the William Clark engravings at Parham Hill, Antigua. It seemed to me that they might complement the photographs in a very special way and throughout the next few years we acquired reproductions of many engravings as well as old maps of Antigua. Gregson agreed to write a text which would set the visual elements in a cultural and historical background. We read the available literature and talked endlessly and, slowly, *Antigua Black* emerged.

In November of 1971 I showed the engravings to Roger Minick, a fellow photographer at the Associated Students' Studio in Berkeley. We talked at length about the book and he became genuinely excited and agreed to work on the project with us. In the course of the next year we selected the photographs and Roger designed a basic layout. When Roger left for his Guggenheim year in photography, Dave Bohn agreed to take over the design and layout and to work with Richard Schuettge on technical production. And so *Antigua Black* finally reached the doors of H. S. Crocker Co., Inc., San Bruno in February 1973.

At the close of a project such as this, there are many things for which one is grateful, but words on paper can hardly serve to convey my appreciation and affection to the many friends who have offered their support and enthusiasm. I hope *Antigua Black* can adequately express my debt to them, but a few friends and relatives should be singled out:

To all of the Davises present at Tanner Street: Mum, Pooks, Auntie, Evie, Vettie, Guy, Junie, Jill, Sally and Graeme, and to those abroad, Ermina and Cecile, all of whom have put up with the distractions of life with a devoted photographer for six summers and one winter, and whose love has provided me with a deeper understanding of the Antiguan people.

To all those Antiguans who let me into their lives—those who were photographed and those who helped me find the photographs, among them Robin Bascus and the Williams family in Bolans. To Mr. Weaver, especially, I owe a great deal. His hospitality towards me has been matched only by his devotion to the great cause of growing the perfect Antigua Black pineapple.

To Betty Cannon whose enthusiasm for my work has been constant and whose timely assistance made it possible for me to photograph the sugar cane harvest in Antigua in February, 1970.

To Willis Van Devanter whose immense love for, and knowledge of, beautiful old books led us into the world of Caribbean color engravings, and whose generosity opened up other worlds as well.

To Ray Baumback and the staff at Bofors, Inc., who outdid themselves in the production of the *Antigua Black* brochure. They set the tone of quality which was to follow.

To the production staff at H. S. Crocker Co., Inc., who grappled with the many technical problems while I looked on with a blend of concern and confidence.

To Teddy Winslow for her steady interest in and support of this project from start to finish.

To the staff and students at the ASUC Studio, Berkeley, for giving the admiration and criticism in the right proportions and with the right spirit, from 1967 to the present.

To Frederick and Greta Mitchell, for keeping Scrimshaw Press so vital and for helping to put *Antigua Black* on the bookshelf.

To Dick Schuettge, whose ideas and suggestions were an important part of the final designing and production, and who was himself an invaluable member of our work crew.

To Roger Minick, whose photographs I admire and who admired mine enough to spend countless hours roughing out the book, producing a lovely brochure, and helping me to select the photographs for *Antigua Black*.

To Dave Bohn who was first my teacher, then friend and mentor, whose sensitive criticism helped to produce the Antigua photographs from the very first images in 1967 right through the years, and whose personal interest has helped transform them from a stack of matted prints into a bound volume.

To Gregson, whose ideas helped to shape this book and without whom there would have been no "Portrait of an Island People."

And to Anika, last only because she is so very special and because her birth came toward the end of this project. May *Antigua Black* help her, as well as other Antiguans, to "know her own history."

MARGO DAVIS

LIST OF REFERENCES

ANDREWS, EVANGELINE, Ed.

1939. *Journal of a Lady of Quality; being the Narrative of a Journey from Scotland to the West Indies, North Carolina, and Portugal in the Years 1774 to 1776*, by Janet Schaw. 3rd ed., New Haven.

BOWEN, EMAN

1750. *A new and accurate map of the Island of Antigua or Antego....*

BRATHWAITE, EDWARD

1969. *Islands*. London.

COHEN, JOHN M.

1969. *The Four Voyages of Christopher Columbus*. Baltimore.

CRUXENT, JOSE MARIA and IRVING ROUSE

1969. "Early Man in the West Indies," *Scientific American* 221:42-52

DAVIES, JOHN

1666. *The History of the Carriby-Islands...*, London (A translation of Louis de Poincy, *Histoire naturelle et morale des Isles Antilles de l'Amerique*, 1658).

DAVIES, K. G., Ed.

1963. "Report to Governor Mathew of an enquiry into the negro conspiracy. Antigua, 30 December 1736," *Calendar of State Papers*, Colonial Series, America and West Indies. vol. 43., London.

EDWARDS, PAUL, Ed.

1967. *Equiano's Travels: His Autobiography: The Interesting Narrative of the Life of Olaudah Equiano or Gustavus Vassa the African.* London.

"FLANNIGAN, MRS."

1844. *Antigua and the Antiguans...* 2 vols., London.

GOVEIA, ELSA V.

1965. *Slave Society in the British Leeward Islands at the end of the Eighteenth Century.* New Haven.

HARRIS, DAVID R.

1965. *Plants, Animals and Man in the Outer Leeward Islands, West Indies.* University of California Publications in Geography, vol. 18, Berkeley.

HIGHAM, CHARLES S. S.

1921. *The Development of the Leeward Islands under the Restoration, 1660-1688.* Cambridge, England.

JANE, CECIL, Translator.

1968. *The Journal of Christopher Columbus.* London.

LUFFMAN, JOHN

1789. *A Brief Account of the Island of Antigua, Together with the Customs and Manners of Its Inhabitants...* London.

MARTIN-KAYE, P.H.A.

1959. *Reports on the Geology of the Leeward and British Virgin Islands.* St. Lucia.

MORISON, SAMUEL ELIOT

1942. *Admiral of the Ocean Sea.* Boston.

MORISON, SAMUEL ELIOT and MAURICIO OBREGON

1964. *The Caribbean as Columbus Saw It.* Boston.

OLIVER, VERE L.

1894-99. *The History of the Island of Antigua From the First Settlement in 1635 to the Present Time.* 3 vols., London.

ROUSE, IRVING

1964. "Prehistory of the West Indies," *Science* 144: 499-513.

SCHULER, MONICA

1970. "Akan Slave Rebellions in the British Caribbean," *Savacou* I:8-31.

SHERIDAN, R. B.

1957. "Letters from a Sugar Plantation in Antigua, 1739-1758," *Agricultural History* 31: 3-23.

Five thousand copies of *Antigua Black* were printed at
H. S. Crocker Co., Inc., in April, 1973. The photographs
are reproduced by double-impression offset lithography on
Warren's Cameo Dull. Composition is by Graham Mackintosh,
Trump Mediaeval throughout. Binding is by Cardoza-James.
Production by Richard Schuettge and Dave Bohn.
Design and layout by Roger Minick and Dave Bohn.